ON

THE STUDY

OF THE

PHILOSOPHY OF THE MIND

AND LOGIC.

ON

THE STUDY

OF THE

PHILOSOPHY OF THE MIND

AND LOGIC.

AN

INTRODUCTORY LECTURE,

DELIVERED IN THE

UNIVERSITY OF LONDON,

ON MONDAY, NOV. 8, 1830.

BY THE REV. JOHN HOPPUS, A. M.

PROFESSOR OF THE PHILOSOPHY OF THE MIND AND LOGIC IN THE
UNIVERSITY OF LONDON.

LONDON:

PRINTED BY THOMAS DAVISON,

FOR JOHN TAYLOR, 30, UPPER GOWER STREET,

BOOKSELLER AND PUBLISHER TO THE UNIVERSITY.

1830.

ON

THE STUDY

OF THE

PHILOSOPHY OF THE MIND

AND LOGIC.

GENTLEMEN,

THE department of education, the honour of teaching which is assigned to me, is The Philosophy of the Human Mind; including Logic; which branch of it immediately relates to the operation of Reasoning, the most distinguished function which belongs to mind.

The term *mind* is so familiar to us in ordinary speech, that it might seem almost superfluous to dwell upon its meaning. It is as frequently upon our lips as the word matter, or body; and so far as all common purposes are concerned, it conveys a signification quite as definite. We speak of matter and of mind with equal familiarity; and we know as clearly what we mean when we say that our minds are *thinking* on any subject, as when we say that a mass of matter, which we term a stone, is falling to the earth, or that our own bodies are moving from one place to another.

If any one, therefore, to whom that interesting and truly useful science which is now before us, is new, should propose the question, *what is mind?* under the impression that it is something which is less capable of being known to us than the objects of matter (an impression not uncommon, probably, to those who are unaccustomed to philosophical reflection) we should deem it the most ready and instructive mode of reply, first to propose another query, and to ask, *what is that which we term matter?*

This question, we are aware, may, at first view, seem much more easy to be answered than the former, which relates to *mind.* There is something so tangible in the various objects that surround us; something so impressive in the colours they reflect to our eyes; something so well-defined in their shapes and outlines, and so distinct in the resistance they present to the grasp of our hands; and, moreover, the greater part of these objects exhibit so considerable a degree of permanence and stability as they exist in space: while, on the other hand, there is something so very fleeting and shadowy in many of our thoughts and inward feelings, that if we have never reflected much on the subject of *matter,* and its properties, we shall scarcely be able, without some effort, to conceive otherwise, than that we have the means of being much more familiarly acquainted with matter than we can hope to be with that invisible, untangible, mysterious something, which thinks, and reasons, and remembers, and hopes, and fears, and to which we give the name of *mind.* A moment's reflection, however, may suffice to convince us that our knowledge of mind is even more immediate and direct than our knowledge of matter, distinct as that knowledge appears to be, since all we know of matter is acquired indirectly, or through the medium of our sensations; whereas, what we know of mind and its faculties arises directly from itself, that is, from the consciousness we feel of what is passing within us.

To the question, *what is matter?* the reply can only be, that matter is a name we assign to a certain assemblage and union of qualities, as they exist in the various objects of the visible world. These objects are composed of something that is extended, shaped into certain forms, of a certain resistance, capable of being divided, and, for the most part, coloured. These qualities exist in union with each other, not only in the largest masses of solid or fluid matter, but even in the smallest microscopic atoms.

If it be again asked, after the above enumeration of qualities, *what is matter?* what is that to which extension, resistance, divisibility belong? what is the *substratum*, as it has been termed, of which all these are the properties? The answer must be, *we know not.* It was supposed, indeed, in the infancy of modern science, that a more intimate acquaintance with the objects of nature, than at that time existed, might lead to the discovery of the *essences*, or, as they were technically called, by a term borrowed from the Platonists, the *forms* of things, or *that* in which the abovenamed properties were supposed to inhere. Lord Bacon, whose vast and sanguine genius poured a flood of new light over the whole field of human knowledge, thought that this ultimate essence or substratum was open to the scrutiny of man, and might be destined, in a more advanced period of science, to become a new trophy to the power of the Inductive Method. Upwards of two centuries, however, have now elapsed, under the auspices of the Baconian philosophy, without any thing being known of this *natura naturans*, as Bacon himself expresses it; the *essence* of matter, or that which constitutes it what it is. Indeed, were any thing further even discovered, relating to matter in general, than we already know, it is difficult to conceive that this could be viewed by us as any thing more than some new quality; or that matter would then be to us more than what it now is; namely, an assemblage and union of properties, one or more being simply added to those we are already acquainted with. We must, therefore, be contented to reply to the question, *what is matter?* that it is that which has certain properties, as extension, figure, resistance, divisibility. In short, we know matter only as an assemblage of qualities or properties, under every modification of it which is presented to our notice.

We are now in a condition to recur to the former question, namely, *what is mind?* And here the reply must be on the very same principle. Mind is known to us in the same manner. It is known by its properties, for which its faculties, powers, susceptibilities, are but other names. Both matter and mind present themselves under the aspect of two distinct sets of qualities, those of matter being the objects of our senses, those of mind the objects of our consciousness. Hence the distinguishing peculiarity, that while *matter* is the mere object of which mind takes cognizance, *mind* is at once the object and the agent, both the observer and the thing observed; in which circumstance much of the difficulty of intellectual science consists, and at the same time much of the utility which it possesses in fixing the attention of the mind upon itself.

As the respective properties of matter and of mind are the only sources of our knowledge regarding them, so those properties with which we are familiar, as belonging to mind, are as *different* as can be imagined from those we assign to matter. We are accustomed, indeed, to apply to mind terms borrowed from matter, in such expressions as *solidity* of judgment, or the more philosophical phrase, *association of ideas*, as though one thought were in some way joined to another. These and many similar expressions, it is obvious, are merely figurative, and are derived, perhaps unavoidably, from the analogy of the properties of matter—expressions, however, some of which, unless we always bear in mind their real value as mere figures, may greatly mislead us in our study of the mental faculties.

It is these faculties or properties alone, we may repeat, that convey to us any notion of mind. As matter, therefore, is the name we give to that which has extension, figure, colour, resistance; so mind is the term by which we call that which has thought, remembrance, reason, joy, grief, love, hate, hope, fear—qualities these which are altogether peculiar and its own, being totally different from those of matter, and having nothing in common with them; for what can be conceived more dissimilar than extension, shape, hardness or softness, on the one hand, and ideas, remembrances, emotions, and volitions, on the other? The entire *unlikeness* which there is between these two separate classes of properties, leads us familiarly to assign to the subjects of them distinct names—*matter* and *mind;* though with regard to any thing beyond their respective properties, as what may be the *nature* or *essence* of either, we are in both cases in the same situation. We know each precisely on the same principle; that is, we know both simply in their properties.

The faculties or states of our consciousness above alluded to, such as imagination, volition, memory, and the like, are readily assigned to mind, as obviously distinguished from the attributes of the matter of which our bodies are composed. There is, however, another class of our states of conscious existence not named with the above, which do not perhaps appear so evidently to be properties of mind: I refer to what we familiarly understand by the term *sensations*. In these there is so much that seems corporeal, that to some it may possibly appear almost inconsistent to term them states of *mind;* while it may be readily admitted that all our other kinds of consciousness are justly entitled to that designation. In what we are accustomed to term a train of thought, for instance, one mental image or picture of fancy succeeds another in the absence of the real external objects of which these ideas seem to be the copies, as is the case in those musings and reveries which frequently occur to all, when the shadows of the past appear to rise again to view, and to give origin to new and successive combinations of what we are conscious to ourselves are strictly mental states, and which are perpetually succeeding each other until they are terminated by some new circumstance, which arises to break the inward spell of imagination, and to call back the mind from this day-dream to the realities of the external world. When Milton, by the magic of his immortal genius, places before our mental view the most beautiful images of nature in all the freshness of the new-born creation — " the breath of morn; the charm of earliest birds; the pleasant sun, with his orient beams; the fragrant and fertile earth; the coming on of evening mild; the silent night, and her

solemn bird; with the fair moon, and glittering starlight—
we do not hesitate for a moment to admit, that the spectral
scene which seems to accumulate before us, and to pass
rapidly over the field of thought within us, is in the utmost
strictness to be denominated a *mental train*. Or, when in
the phenomena of *dreaming*, the mind seems to assert her
independence of the organs of sense and of the outward universe, and to exercise her powers in mystic and enchanted
scenes of her own creation, producing more vivid and di-
versified pictures than any voluntary effort of imagination
can command, while the images of fancy succeed each other
in what appears to us, on the review of them in our waking
moments, a capricious and casual assemblage—though even
these are probably all regulated by the great fundamental
law of association;—when, as one of the most sentimental
of our poets describes this mysterious phænomenon of
dreaming—

> " The soul fantastic measures treads
> O'er fairy fields, or mourns along the gloom
> Of pathless woods, or down the craggy steep
> Hurl'd headlong, swims with pain the mantled pool,
> Or scales the cliff,"

we at once refer the process to the mind itself, and we are
conscious that the whole is an affection of that same being
which carries on endless trains of imagination in our waking
hours. All these successive states of consciousness we perceive to be one remove at least from every thing that we
could suppose to be merely corporeal. In the case, however, of what we term our *sensations*, which we feel to be
so much more evidently involved in our bodily frame than
the former, we may at first view almost have the impression
that these are rather to be regarded as states of *body* than
of mind. The sensation we feel, for example, on the application of vinegar to the tongue, or of a strong electric spark
to any part of the body, or in the disorganization of its

texture by a burn or a laceration, may seem less properly to be denominated a *mental* state or affection than those above alluded to.

A little reflection, however, may suffice to convince us that our sensations, though they are more obviously connected with our bodily frame than our other states of consciousness, are, ultimately, not less truly to be regarded as states of mind. Sensation, as the attribute of a sentient being, is as different from any of the attributes or qualities we usually ascribe to matter, as even thoughts or emotions themselves. We never suppose for a moment that a stone or a piece of wood, nor have we evidence that even a tree, though it is endowed with vegetable life, has any thing that can properly be termed sensation, any more than that it is capable of a train of imagery, or of the emotions of sublimity and beauty; and we should be as ready to smile at the philosopher who gravely told us that the blade of grass we tread on, or the stone against which we stumble, felt a sensation of pain, as if he affirmed that the very same blade or the same stone felt emotions of anger and resentment at being thus trampled on and made our footstool. What we term matter, gives no indications of any such sensations, and when our own organized frame is dead, sensation becomes extinct.

It is true, indeed, from the discoveries of anatomy and physiology, that our sensations are directly and immediately connected with what is termed the *nervous system*, that is, with the brain and that appendage or prolongation of it which is produced along the spine, and distributed in innumerable ramifications to every part of the body, and which is especially determined to the organs of sense. It is generally admitted, that when these nerves or filaments are divided, so as to interrupt probably some unknown mode of communication with the cerebral mass, there is then no sensation in the part below them to which they belong. The fact, however, that the process of sensation is dependent on the nervous system, does not prove that sensation is entirely or ultimately corporeal, since it is well known that our trains of thought and our emotions have a considerable degree of dependence on the existing state of the body. The train of ideas in which the fancy is apt to run, and the tempers and feelings which the mind is most wont to cherish, are greatly modified for the time being by the state of the digestive organs, and of the health in general. All this indicates that the mind is influenced to a considerable extent by the condition of the body, and may, perhaps, even authorise us to term the brain the great general organ of the mind. It is, however, the mysterious and un-known union of our material frame with that which is capable of thought, which renders us susceptible of *sensation*, and it is ultimately the same being which has sensations, which also possesses ideas, will, passions; or, in other words, all sensation is ultimately in the mind.

The language, moreover, which nature dictates, when we speak of ourselves, evidently flows from the certain conscious-ness we feel that it is the same *I* who have *sensations*— suppose those arising from an air played on a musical in-strument, who also have the recurrence of something like these sensations after they have died away; as when we say, " I hear the air," and " I remember the air." This language seems to indicate the irresistible consciousness we feel that we who are the subjects of remembrance, and of other in-tellectual functions, are also the subjects of those sensations about which we are capable of exercising memory or reason.

Regarding mind, therefore, as the only ultimate object of all our states of consciousness, of whatever kind, it is separated from mere matter by a broad line of demarcation. Matter has colour, extension, resistance; and if divided into any number of parts, it still possesses, in each part, the same general properties which it possessed in that mass which, to our perceptions, before its division, conveyed the notion of unity. Mind has sensations, thoughts, volitions, emotions, judgments, and these are indivisible; for how absurd should we at once feel it to be, apart from all figurative language, to talk of half an idea, one fourth part of a sensation, or the one-third of a volition !

All those properties, therefore, which we are conscious of possessing, that have no resemblance to the general properties of the material objects that surround us, we assign to *mind;* and it is a fact worthy to be remarked, that, amidst all the changes which our bodies may undergo, we possess an irresistible consciousness of the *identity* or *sameness* of our minds. Whatever difficulties may attach to the identity of our bodily frame at different periods of its existence, *that* which thinks and reasons, and hopes and fears, still continues to exist unchanged in these various and everflowing states of consciousness; and we possess a uniform and irresistible impression, not dependent on reasoning, and incapable of being strengthened by it, that this thinking being, our mind, is always the same; that all we strictly mean by the term *I* is the same now that it was in our childhood, and that the identical being which had certain thoughts, and feelings, and emotions, in time past, is now actually remembering these various states of former consciousness.

The very idea of remembrance includes the idea that it is *we* who remember. The assertion, I *remember*, takes for granted the identity of that which remembers, and involves the intuitive consciousness of one permanent self, which remains the same amidst all the endless fluctuation of its own thoughts and feelings. Hence, though remembrance is not the proof of mental identity, which is incapable of being subjected to proof, yet remembrance seems essential to our conception of the idea of self, which idea identity involves; for if we suppose a mind totally destitute of memory, such a mind could possess no consciousness but of the present instant; it would be alike cut off from the past and from the future, for our anticipations of the future can only arise from our knowledge of the past. It is difficult, therefore, to imagine how a mind thus supposed to be destitute of memory, could have the notion of a permanent self, which is the one subject of those states of consciousness that were existing some time ago, and of those which are now present.

Whatever we may think of the changes which the bodily frame undergoes, those changes to which mind is subject cannot be conceived as at all affecting its substantial identity. Even matter itself exhibits certain changes which we never regard as impairing its real sameness. A pith ball is the same ball, whether it be charged with electricity, attracting and repelling other bodies, or in its natural state; and a planet is the same identical mass, whether in its aphelion or its perihelion, though in these situations it is in very different positions, and is very different in its state with reference to gravity. As matter may thus undergo certain relative changes without its identity being impaired, so there is no reason to suppose that the same may not be the case with regard to mind itself. The mind, in childish ignorance, or in high cultivation, or in its more fleeting aspects of sensation, intellect, or emotion, is certainly in states that are very different from each other; none of these, however, seem incompatible with the real identity of what we may term the substance of mind.

It is remarkable that Mr. Locke, in his Essay on the Human Understanding, makes the identity of mind not merely to be *ascertained* to us by our own consciousness, but actually to *consist* in it. He states that this identity consists " not in the identity of substance," but in the " identity of consciousness," by which here he must mean remembrance; and he makes the following singular supposition and remark : " If Socrates waking and Socrates sleeping do not partake of the same consciousness, Socrates waking and sleeping is not the same person." " Mr. Locke's observations on this subject," observes that acute and profound reasoner, Bishop Butler, " appear to be hasty." " Though consciousness (remembrance) of what is past," continues this celebrated writer, " does thus *ascertain* our identity to ourselves, yet to say that it *makes* identity, or is necessary to our being the same persons, is to say that a person has not existed a single moment, nor done one action but what he can remember *."

We have all along spoken of that which thinks, or mind, as so remarkably different, in its properties, from matter, as to present a ground of distinction quite sufficient for all the common purposes of life. We may even go further, and remark, that the philosophy of mind might be substantially conducted apart from any opinions as to the *nature* of mind itself; for this philosophy chiefly consists in the observation, the registry, the arrangement, the succession, and so far as it can be carried, the analysis of its various faculties, states, or phenomena. The subject of the *immateriality* of mind, so far as it can become a topic of speculation by reason, may, as to its detail, be deferred with propriety, till after we have become more familiar with the actual and innumerable facts which mind exhibits to our consciousness and observation. Though we know nothing, however, either of matter or of mind, but the properties which each exhibits to us, yet we can scarcely dwell, even for a moment, on the phenomena of mind, without almost involuntarily drawing a comparison between them and the facts of the material universe. All we *do* know of mind is so totally unlike all we do know of matter, that we have the strongest presumption from analogy that what is hidden from our view in regard to mind, is equally different from that which also may remain unknown to us in reference to matter. If we may with any propriety use such terms as *essence, nature, substratum,* as names for that unknown something to which material properties belong, and also for that other unknown something to which mental properties belong, we are strongly led to believe that these respective *essences* or *substances* must be as different from each other, in the order of being, as the properties are different which we assign to each; and that if one is to be denominated matter, the other is *not* matter, which is all that we can mean by the epithet *immaterial.*

The indivisibility and oneness moreover of which we are

* Butler's Analogy.

conscious in all our mental operations, and to which allusion has previously been made, presents an additional point of dissimilarity between the properties of matter and those of mind. Extension, figure, solidity, viewed as attributes of matter, can be divided indefinitely; but belief, surprise, imagination, in short all our thoughts and feelings are strictly indivisible; and the very supposition of any one of the various modes of consciousness which are incident to a conscious mind being divided into separate portions of consciousness, opposes this very consciousness. The body after death ceases to exist as one mass, and though its particles are not destroyed, there is a dissolution of their continuity; but we have no evidence for believing that the integrity and identity of mind are affected by this change to which the mere body is destined; or that mind ceases to possess all those faculties which are not entirely dependent on the body for their exercise, as is obviously the case with *sensation.* Had we, therefore, no clearer light than reason can afford, though we could never probably have arrived at any very *positive* and *direct* evidence for the immateriality of mind, or even for the still more interesting fact of its immortality; yet there would appear a considerable presumption from analogy, where analogy could be our only guide, that mind might exist apart from all that is visible of man; and might be destined to survive, in some new mode of existence, the dissolution and the wreck of that corporeal machinery to which it is now so closely and so mysteriously united.

The remarks which have hitherto been made, include some topics which may with propriety be deferred in the class, to a future period of the course, as being less adapted to the elementary part of instruction than many other subjects in the fertile field of the intellectual philosophy.

I shall now proceed to advert to the principles on which the study of the philosophy of mind should be conducted. And here we cannot too much admire the spirit of that method of investigating nature, which, indeed, was in every age the secret and presiding genius which produced all, in philosophy, that could survive the lapse of time, and the progress of the human intellect, but which was first distinctly embodied in a systematic form by Bacon, in those great works in which he sketched the grand, rude outlines of all human knowledge; and traced that career of advancement which, in modern times, has been entered on by the mind of man with such brilliant success. In natural science the period of hypothetical fancies, and the dominion of names, is now past; and the darkness of the middle ages has fled before the light of rational inquiry. By the accurate and patient observation of nature, the foundation has been laid for the whole superstructure of modern science, and the grand fundamental principle which was laid down by the gifted father of the experimental philosophy, is now generally admitted; namely, that " man being nothing more, as an inquirer after knowledge, than the minister and interpreter of nature, knows nothing but what he is able actually to observe of the appearances which nature exhibits to his view." It was the neglect of this great principle, as applied to the philosophy of mind, that left an uncertainty and a darkness hanging over it, long after the advantages of following so rational a method had begun to develop themselves, in the achievements of natural science.

It must be the aim, therefore, of the inquirer in intellectual philosophy to assimilate, as far as possible, his mode of investigation to that which has proved so eminently successful in the various branches of physical knowledge. Attention to nature and to fact, has proved the key which has unlocked the entrance to the temple of all material science, and revealed its arcana to the view of man; and the same attention to nature and to fact, as existing in the consciousness of our own and other minds, must be our guide in this philosophy, if we would arrive at truth, and claim for our pursuits the designation and the rank of science.

What wonders has not this simple principle of philosophical induction achieved in the *classification* of our knowledge of visible nature! The material universe presents to the eye of the rustic and untaught peasant nothing of that orderly arrangement which modern science has pointed out, and has placed as the basis of its systems. With the exception of a few splendid and striking appearances, such as day and night, and the seasons, there is to the unskilled observer little else than a chaotic mass of stars sparkling in the mighty vault that is above him, distinguished only by their different magnitudes and degrees of brightness; and on the earth, nothing but a confused collection of plants and stones: nor has it ever entered his imagination how the patient research of minds, not more gifted than his own, probably, in natural endowments, has from all this confusion educed the sciences of astronomy, botany, mineralogy, or chymistry. Scarcely less irregularity and disorder do the phenomena of the human mind present to him, who merely gives a cursory glance at those endless and ever-changing aspects which mind exhibits to our consciousness. The principle of classification, therefore, must, as far as possible, be applied to the various facts and laws which occur in the operations of our intellectual nature; and in general, the more we can succeed in imbibing the same spirit which has done so much in the world of matter, as witnessed in the Newtonian system of the universe, in the regeneration of chymistry, and in other results connected with the science of visible nature—the more we can avoid mere hypothesis and establish facts, the more likely shall we be to know all that is within our reach relating to that invisible world of mind, which is so interesting to our curiosity, as immediately comprising the knowledge of ourselves.

There have, no doubt, been systems of intellectual philosophy, which have proved more dazzling to the imagination than one that might seek to rear itself on the basis of a truly philosophical induction. Such systems, however, have owed more to the genius of their authors, and to their poetic effect upon the fancy, than to any appeal which they have made to human consciousness. The romance and sentimentalism, or the over-wrought refinement, that have pervaded the theories which have emanated from some of the continental schools, notwithstanding the talented names that have sometimes thrown a lustre over them, have failed to take a lasting hold on mankind, or to produce a satisfactory conviction in minds that have previously been disciplined in the school of the exact sciences, and that have bowed to the authority of their demonstrations. The philosophy of mind has, in consequence, not unfrequently been regarded as a mere speculation, founded on no solid basis, and has not obtained the justice which is due to its importance and its usefulness, when viewed in its real character. The only hope of rescuing it from the charge of its being a mere hypothesis, adorned with the gaudy colours of fiction and romance, and fitter to be the day-dream of a poetic fancy, than an object of serious attention to the philosopher of modern times—the only chance of its being regarded, not as a pedantic jargon of technical and scholastic phraseology, but as a system of truth which approves itself to our consciousness, is to be found in conducting it, as strictly as possible, on the principles of the Baconian philosophy. As the astronomer has noted and registered the appearances of the heavenly bodies, and as the chymist has analysed the substances of the material world, and enumerated and classified the actual facts which have developed themselves to his attention, till a *theory*, or, according to the etymology of the word, a *view* simply, of these facts, as they all lie before him, has presented itself to his notice; so must the philosopher of mind endeavour as much as possible to proceed in his observations, his arrangement, his analysis of the phenomena, or, which is the same thing, the faculties and susceptibilities of the human mind.

The simplest view which it seems possible to take of the mental faculties, or powers, or operations in general, is to regard them as nothing more than the *mind itself* existing in these various states; some of these states being very simple, as, for instance, all our *sensations*, considered in themselves; other states being more or less complex, and admitting of a sort of relative or virtual analysis, as is the case in many of our ideas and emotions. Thus, the idea we attach to the term *weight* is highly complex, consisting of a number of elementary ideas, which all go as it were to make up the compound idea of *weight*. When we speak of the *weight* of a body, we include, for instance, the idea of resistance, and *that* resistance in a given direction; while the idea of *direction* itself involves the ideas of extension, of place, and of motion: the idea of *will* also is a part of the whole. All these ideas might be shown to be included in the complex idea which is expressed by the term *weight*.

This general view of the faculties and operations of the mind, as being simply the mind in so many distinct states, may be familiarly illustrated by a reference to the various postures of the body. Sitting, standing, and lying down, or stretching out the arm, are not any thing apart from the body itself, or any thing additional to it, but simply the body in these various positions or states; so sensation, memory, will, joy, surprise, admiration, are nothing more than the mind existing in these several states. They are, if we may be allowed to use a figure, the mind in its *different postures*. Each power or faculty, regarded as in actual exercise, is the mind itself in a particular state, or affected in a particular manner.

The common name for all these states of mind is the general term *consciousness*. For to say that we are conscious of having any sensation, conscious of remembering some past event, or conscious of feeling a present emotion, simply means in strictness that we *do* feel that emotion, that we do remember that event, or that we do feel that sensation. Hence a distinguished living writer on the analysis of the human mind, and whose statements are remarkable for their clearness, observes, " The words *conscious* and *consciousness* are *generical* marks, under which all the names of the subordinate classes of the feelings of a sentient creature are included: when I smell a rose, I am conscious; when I remember, I am conscious; when I believe, I am conscious."

Various other terms that are in common use, but which, as applied to intellectual philosophy, will require some explanation, will be noticed as they arise in the course of lecturing, with a view to give as much precision as possible to the meaning of words, and to the ideas which the student attaches to them. Some of these definitions will involve important doctrines in the science of mind, as is the case with regard to the terms *cause* and *effect*, which, if we analyze the ideas that are associated with them, will be found, ultimately, to signify nothing more, as to our knowledge, than simple antecedence or priority in time, in the one case, and simple subsequence in the other. The term *power* also simply means the *invariableness* and *uniformity* of this same antecedence and this same subsequence; for if we say that the fluoric acid has the *power* of dissolving *silex*, this is the same thing as saying that this acid always *does*, according to experience, dissolve silex, when the latter is subjected to its action. And if we further say, as though by way of accounting for the fact, that the acid is *adapted* to dissolve the silex, this is truly nothing more than the expression of our *expectation of the future* from the experience of the past; or, in other words, that since the fluoric acid always has dissolved flint, it always will dissolve it. These terms, in short, express, in strictness, nothing more than our experience of the ordinary laws which the Creator has established in the government of the physical world, and which to our faculties are simply known as different series of events, one of which succeeds another in uniform order.

In regard to the classification of the phenomena of mind, it may be remarked that man has always been considered, even by the earliest philosophers, as at once a *sentient*, an *intellectual*, and a *moral* being. Hence, apart from the consideration of the faculty of sensation, philosophy was very anciently divided into two parts, namely, the *contemplative* and the *active*. At a subsequent period, a similar division of intellectual philosophy obtained for many ages, in which were treated the operations of the *Understanding*, and those

C

of the *Will.* The more modern phraseology of the *Intellectual* and *Active Powers*, amounts nearly to the same, consisting only in a change of terms. This division, however, we may venture to remark, is exceedingly liable to mislead us; for if all our more strictly mental faculties, or states of consciousness, be reduced to the general classes of understanding and will, how are we to arrange such inward feelings as joy, sorrow, hope, fear, in short all our affections and emotions; which, as they are not sensations, so also evidently include more than belongs to the mere province of the understanding or intellect; and which at the same time are not in many cases subject to the will, since they often exist independently of our volitions, and even in opposition to our utmost voluntary efforts. Or if we term our passions and emotions *active powers*, may not the mind be said to be equally active in the use of reason, or in those rapid and unbidden trains of imagination which succeed each other by the laws of association? Reason and imagination, however, in themselves considered, are uniformly regarded as intellectual powers. What then, in this view, we may ask, becomes of the division into *intellectual and active powers?*

A preferable division probably is the arrangement of the whole mass of our states of conscious existence, that is, the whole of our powers, faculties, or susceptibilities, the mental phenomena in general, into the following classes; namely, I. *Sensations;* II. *Intellectual States*, of which the chief element are ideas; and III. *Emotions.*

I. The most simple and obvious of our modes of consciousness consist of the *first* of these three general divisions, that is, *Sensations*, or sensitive states of mind, including all those feelings which we have immediately through the medium of our bodily frame. These, therefore, will first come under consideration.

1. The most familiar of them are those which we possess by means of the organs of sense, which may therefore be termed our *organic sensations*, as in *smell, taste, hearing, touch,* and *vision.*

2. Next are those sensations which may be denominated *muscular*, or those which are connected with the action of the various muscles of the animal frame; and which arise from our voluntary motions, or from the property of *resistance* in matter. It is from this very important, though often neglected, order of sensations, that we derive our idea of *externality*, or of the existence of objects external to the mind; also our idea of some of the properties and relations of material objects which are commonly ascribed to vision.

3. There are also other feelings, which we may term *Internal Sensations*; such are the appetites of hunger and thirst. Other and less definite internal feelings are connected with some of the functions essential to life, as those belonging to the stomach in digestion; also those inward sensations which sometimes follow, and seem to blend themselves with the emotions of the mind, as in fear, alarm, etc., when there is a reaction, as it were, of the mind upon the body, and a sensation more or less definite is felt about the region of the heart.

It is probable, that to one or other of these three orders, or to some combination of them, the whole mass of our ordinary sensations may be assigned.

4. There remain only what we may term *morbid* or *accidental* sensations, such as those which arise from a morbid state of the organs of sense, or from external injuries producing a greater or less disorganization of the parts; also those internal sensations which are peculiar to various diseases. To this last class also may be referred all our sensations of pain and fatigue.

II. The second general division of all our states or modes of consciousness, includes all that are not sensations on the one hand, or emotions, which constitute the third class, on the other. These we may term the more strictly *Intellectual States* of mind, including all our ideas, and all our purely intellectual operations. This second department, as it is the widest, so it is the most difficult in the philosophy of the mind, since it furnishes the principal field for distinction and analysis, and is every where so greatly influenced by the associating principle.

The most leading fact in reference to this second general division of our consciousness, the more strictly intellectual part of our nature, is that *ideas* are here the chief elements; for in all our intellectual states of mind these are involved. It is a familiar circumstance in the history of mind, that in the absence of sensations, and of the external objects which excite them, we can have what seems a kind of shadow, or likeness of them in the mind. We appear almost to see again some object that we have before actually beheld, when that object is no longer present; the musical sounds and harmonies that we have previously heard, seem to be heard again, after they have ceased; and the same recurrence of something which is a kind of representation of our past sensations, may to a certain extent be traced in regard to our remaining senses. These mental images of the past, as we may figuratively term them, whether they are simple copies of our actual sensations, or imaginary combinations of them, may be called *sensible ideas.* Other ideas, which are not immediate resemblances, and combinations of sensations may be distinguished by the term *mental or abstract ideas.* Such are the idea of goodness, the idea of government, and in general the ideas which are suggested by the names we give to all intellectual and moral qualities.

One idea, moreover, may suggest another; thus the idea of Egypt may be instantly followed by ideas of the pyramids. Hence the phrase with which all are familiar, the Association of Ideas—a fact, in the history of the mental phenomena, which meets us in some form or other at every step of our inquiries; and which may be said to have almost the same relation to mind, which the grand law of physical attraction bears to matter. It is not, however, ideas alone that are capable of suggesting or calling up each other. The sound of a person's name, which is a sensation, produces, as it were, a picture of the absent individual in the mind, in which case the association is between a sensation and an idea.

Again, the idea of some particular individual, or of some event, may awaken some emotion : thus, the idea of a person who has done us a kindness may excite a renewal of that gratitude which we may have formerly felt, and the association is now between an idea and an emotion. Hence the more general term *association* may be regarded as preferable to the phrase association of ideas, which seems to limit this grand pervading mental principle to the connexion of *ideas* only among themselves.

This great fundamental law of association did not escape the discriminating notice of Aristotle; who, aware of its importance and influence, especially points it out in our voluntary efforts to recollect what we have forgotten. In his Treatise on Memory, he lays down three laws of association, which very nearly resemble those stated many ages after by Mr. Hume. Aristotle observes, that " we hunt for the idea we are in quest of among other ideas, either of present or former objects, καὶ αφ' 'ομοίου, ἢ ἐναντίου, ἢ τοῦ συνέγγυς ; also from their resemblance, or contrast, or proximity."

For the exhibition of the importance and the all-pervading influence of association, we are, in more modern times, greatly indebted to Dr. Hartley; who has, however, blended his speculations on it with the fanciful and now exploded hypothesis of *vibrations*, which he considers as necessary to every mental affection. More recently, the doctrine of association has been applied with much philosophical acumen to the analysis of several of the intellectual faculties, which had usually been considered as entirely distinct and simple powers, by the late Dr. Thomas Brown of Edinburgh, a philosopher whose name it would here be unpardonable not to mention ; and whose acute and splendid productions have commanded admiration in proportion as they have been known ; a man, the qualities of whose intellect were only exceeded by those of his heart, and who was worthy to be the successor of Dugald Stewart, as one of the great masters and improvers of intellectual science, on the sound principles of the inductive philosophy. It was the opinion of Dr. Brown that all our associations might, by a very fine analysis, be ultimately traced to some prior co-existence of ideas, or of other states of consciousness. If the analysis here alluded to be correct, the term *association* would simply express a fact. It would, however, only express the fact of the co-existence of these ideas or feelings: it does not express their succession. It may therefore, perhaps, in many cases, be preferable, with the above distinguished philosopher, to employ the term *suggestion;* as, for instance, when we say that one idea is associated with another, we often mean merely to state the fact that, *under certain circumstances*, one idea precedes or suggests another, or stands to it in the relation of antecedent.

What these circumstances are, or, in other words, what are the principal *laws* or *facts* relating to Association or Suggestion, will form a very important and interesting part of the studies of the class.

Next will come to be considered the various intellectual faculties themselves, or those phenomena of mind which are usually so denominated.

Before going very minutely into the analysis of these intellectual phenomena, it may be proper to notice them chiefly as they are commonly enumerated, and to describe and distinguish them; so that the student may become familiar with the principal facts relating to them, and may be better prepared for afterwards inquiring whether they can be referred to still more general principles.

In this part of the subject, therefore, will be treated— Consciousness; Perception; Conception; Reflection; Imagination; Memory; Habit and Instinct; the Process of Naming, together with the Use of Language in General, as an Instrument of Thought; Classification and Abstraction; Judgment; Belief; Reasoning. Here also may be noticed some other topics, which may be viewed, as partly holding of intellect, and partly of emotion; as, Attention; Taste, as applied to the Mind; and Conscience.

This part of the course will also be the proper place for the introduction of LOGIC, which is included under *reasoning,* or *ratiocination*, since it relates to the analysis of this process of the mind. Logic is not, as has been often erroneously supposed, a peculiar *method* of reasoning, but is the method which must be virtually adopted in all reasoning that is conclusive and correct. The *syllogism* is the simplest case of reasoning; and every piece of argument is capable of being expanded into a number of syllogisms, each syllogism constituting one distinct and separate link of the whole chain.

The extravagant praise and the absurd application of the Grecian Logic, which prevailed for many ages, have produced that reaction against it which may be regarded as the opposite extreme. As a discipline of the mind, and a part of the analysis of its functions, it may fairly claim a place in the Intellectual Philosophy. "The technical language connected with it," says Mr. Stewart, in the second volume of his Elements, "is now so incorporated with all the higher departments of learning, that, independently of any consideration of its practical applications, some knowledge of its peculiar phraseology may be regarded as an indispensable preparation both for scientific and literary pursuits. To the philosopher it must ever remain a subject of speculation peculiarly interesting, as one of the most singular facts in the history of the human understanding. The ingenuity and subtlety of the invention, and the comprehensive reach of thought displayed in the systematic execution of so vast a design, form a proud and imperishable monument to the powers of Aristotle's mind."

Such a portion of time will be devoted in the class to the *analysis* and exemplification of the Aristotelian Logic as may be deemed best calculated to promote the leading design of the whole course, namely, the intellectual improvement of the student, and the most useful and efficient exercise of the faculties of his mind, as preparatory to his future pursuits in life.

As connected with reasoning, several collateral topics of importance will also be considered; as, the mode of acquiring, recording, and communicating knowledge; the experimental or inductive method of inquiry, as treated by Bacon; with especial reference to the more practical parts of the *Novum Organum*; synthesis and analysis; hypothesis and theory; *à priori* and *à posteriori* reasoning; and Evidence in general.

After these topics have exercised the attention of the student, we may next consider how far the leading faculties of the mind, as above enumerated, may be regarded as capable of being reduced, according to the views of some philosophers, to the two mere simple faculties of Memory and Judgment.

This subject may be further pursued in the inquiry, whether the same mental functions can be resolved yet more generally, by an analysis that is still more recondite, on the principle of association or suggestion.

III. We may now proceed to the third and last of those classes into which all our consciousness was divided; namely, Emotions. These will be readily distinguished, both from sensations and from the strictly intellectual faculties. *Rejoicing* and *sorrowing*, *loving* and *hating*, are, it is obvious, very different from *seeing* and *hearing*, and from all other kinds of sensation. They are also very distinct from *remembering* and *reasoning*, and from all the other modifications of intellect. They form a distinct and separate class, and are, in many respects, by far the most interesting and important part of our mental constitution, being the immediate ingredients in happiness or misery, and having a direct bearing on our moral condition.

A being whose existence is chiefly sensitive possesses but a brutal life; and if we could conceive of one that is simply intellectual, and destitute of all capacity for affection and emotion, this being would seem to us little more than a cold abstraction of existence, a Niobe, so to speak, in the moral world, a mere statue of humanity, which, however admirable within the limits of its own excellence, is, nevertheless, like the antiques of the Grecian chisel, correct in outline, but without life and without a heart.

If the comparison that has already been suggested between the grand law of mental association and the great principle of attraction in the material world be at all appropriate, the mind's capability of emotion may be termed the principle of attraction in the *moral* universe, the great law which gives man influence over man, the pervading element of all social and political existence.

It is this capability which gives the chief interest to the contemplation of man's nature. The emotions, affections, and passions of the human mind constitute the springs and the movements of his moral being, corresponding to the forces and motions of the visible world. The material universe, with all its vastness and magnificence, would, without those unceasing movements which seem to form its life and spirit, and which indicate the everlasting, though unseen presence of a presiding and all-pervading Divinity, be destitute of half its power to interest the imagination. It would prove comparatively but a dull and lifeless panorama. It is the *motions* that are always going on in animated nature, the movements of the celestial bodies, the flow of rivers, the waving foliage of the vegetable world to the winds and zephyrs, the thunders of heaven, and the surges of the ocean, that give life and beauty, and energy and grandeur to the whole scene of all that is visible to the eye; and it is the affections, and emotions, and passions of the human soul which give the most profound interest to the contemplation of the intellectual and moral world; since it is on these, on the objects to which they are related and directed, and on the manner in which they are exercised on those objects, that man's happiness depends—that grand and leading pursuit in which he is perpetually engaged. His emotions and his passions are the ultimate elements, of which all his faculties that are merely intellectual are but the antecedents, and they either prove a mild and steady light, which diffuses peace and satisfaction through his own bosom, and on all within his sphere, or become the darkness and the storms, the earthquakes and the conflagrations of his moral hemisphere; diffusing mischief, like the desolations of nature, not only through their own immediate locality, but over all to whom their effects can extend; as Seneca finely describes the insatiableness of ambition, which is like a fire that burns with more violence the more fuel it receives; " ut flammæ, infinitò acrior vis est, quo ex majore incendio emicuit."

The Emotions will first be brought under the student's notice, as regards the description of them, and their various degrees, and modifications, as expressed by different terms; thus, for instance, joy, cheerfulness, contentment, may be viewed as various gradations of the same elementary feeling.

Under the head of Emotions, the *Will* is also to be considered, together with the doctrine of motives, and of the freedom of volition.

The Classification of the Emotions and their Analysis will also here be included.

Some attention may also be paid, in conclusion, to certain other topics, as the original diversity of mind; genius; the merits of the system of phrenology; and the immateriality of mind.

An outline of the principal subjects of the course is given in the Prospectus that has been printed for the use of the class.

The method which will be pursued in teaching the Philosophy of the Mind and Logic will not consist in merely lecturing, which, as the subject must be presumed to be new to the greater part of students, would be imperfect without the addition of much by way of practice. Should there hereafter be a demand for it, by persons who are more advanced, an additional and separate course of *lectures* only may probably be given; but in the present instance the Intellectual Philosophy will be taught as a constituent branch of elementary education, by constantly prescribing short themes, or essays; and by examining the student on the matter which has previously been given him by way of lecture. This method will tend to fix in his mind the general principles and the details of mental science, and will accustom him to the invaluable habit of comparing what is delivered with what passes within his own mind, and of exercising his powers in a manner that cannot fail to be of the highest use to him; in sharpening and strengthening his mind, as the grand instrument that is to be employed in the whole business of his future life, whatever may be the profession to which he may devote himself.

On this principle he will derive benefit even from those parts of the philosophy of mind which are viewed in somewhat different lights by those who have most studied them; and he will exemplify a remark that has been made with great truth, and with felicity of application, to the effect, " that the student of intellectual science, even where he may fail of entire success in his search after truth, will still resemble the votaries of the chase, who derive great benefit from the exercise they take in the pursuit, even when they fail of the game." In this way the student, without any great demand upon his time, will acquire the habit of minutely and closely dwelling on his own thoughts and feelings, and a facility of recording them in writing, in the form of brief remarks, or essays, which will be afterwards publicly brought forward in the class. He will thus, also, prepare himself for entering the arena of honourable emulation at the end of the session, with the view of distinguishing himself by those prizes and honours which will be awarded to merit.

This method of perpetually reducing knowledge to practice, while it enters deeply into the system of education which is adopted in this University in general, and approves itself to every reflecting mind, has also the suffrage of the most enlightened men, both of ancient and modern times. Aristotle regarded philosophy as consisting in the formation of intellectual and moral habits, which were to be acquired by a regular routine of mental discipline: and Quintilian, the great Roman master of education, adopted as a part of his system the plan of prescribing to the pupil a series of themes and exercises, some of the topics of which he has himself left on record. Dr. Barrow, who possessed the distinguished honour of being the preceptor of Newton, remarks, that the " *communication* of truth is only one half of the business of educations." " The most important part," he adds, " is the habit of employing, to some good purpose, the acquisitions of memory, by the exercise of the understanding about them ; and till this be acquired, the acquisition will not be found of much use." And Locke, who may be pronounced the father of the intellectual philosophy, since the revival of learning, has the following important observations in his Essay on the Human Understanding : " Nobody has made any thing by the hearing of rules, or laying them up in his memory; practice must settle the habit of doing without reflecting on the rule ; and you may as well expect to make a good painter or musician extempore, by a lecture or instruction in the arts of music and painting, as a coherent thinker, or strict reasoner, by a set of rules, showing him wherein right reason consists. The faculties of the soul are improved and made useful to us just after the same manner as our bodies are. Would you have a man perform any mechanical operation dexterously and with ease, let him have ever so much vigour, suppleness, and address, yet nobody expects this from him unless he has been used to it, and has employed time and pains in fashioning and forming his hand, or other parts, to these motions. Just so it is in the mind." That in these and similar remarks, both of those ancient and modern writers, who have been in their day the great lights of mankind, there is much important truth, as applied to elementary education in general, we cannot doubt.

It is unnecessary, after what has already been advanced, to detain this audience by any lengthened observations on the practical utility of the philosophy of mind. It cannot, however, be denied, that this branch of knowledge has not yet fully obtained that rank in the systems of education that have been followed in this country which is justly its due. This may in a great measure be attributed to its being too often confounded with those absurd and frivolous pursuits, which wearied the attention of the scholastic philosophers, and on which the regeneration of science has cast so deserved and lasting an odium. These philosophers, not content with inquiring into properties and facts in general, the only sphere that is adapted to the faculties of man, laboured to ascend into the clouds of untangible speculation, and exhausted their powers in dogmatizing on subjects which must necessarily elude the grasp of the human mind. Instead of exercising that independence of thought which bows only to evidence and truth, they became slaves to opinions not their own. The jargon which they handed down from one age to another, and the absurdities which they dignified with the name of science, have in later times rendered the very term " metaphysics" but a watchword for ridicule and contempt; and in this obloquy the inductive philosophy of the mind has most unjustly shared; though we may fairly assert that, when properly conducted, no pursuit is more adapted to produce those correct and active habits of mind which are of the most incalculable use on the great theatre of human life. The direct tendency of the study of the intellectual philosophy is, to induce a just estimate of our mental constitution itself; to lead to profound and correct thinking on all subjects; to produce accuracy and precision in the use of language, and in communicating our ideas to others; to improve taste; to originate a facility of distinguishing where distinction is of the utmost importance; and, in short, to cultivate, and discipline, and invigorate faculties which might otherwise lie partially dormant, from being overlooked and unexercised; and to train the whole energy of our intellectual nature to its most efficient use. These are objects which are too evidently important to require further illustration.

In the universities of North Britain, the philosophy of mind has long maintained the rank of one of the most valuable and popular branches of education; and its successful cultivators in that country, following the impulse originally given by the immortal Locke in England, may, with him, claim a place among the benefactors of mankind. Of this number are such philosophers as Reid, Stewart, and Brown. The light which those great schools in which the intellectual philosophy has so long reigned, have reflected on the public mind in that country, may be seen, we may venture to say, in no inconsiderable degree, in the habits of superior intelligence which mark the general population, in which they are probably not equalled by any nation in Europe. The institution of a class for the cultivation of this branch of science by the founders of this University, may be regarded as a happy omen that it will in future be more duly appreciated in this country; for there is little doubt that time only is wanting to produce the general conviction of its claim to attention as a branch of elementary education, by furnishing here the opportunity of that actual experience of its benefits, to which all who have devoted themselves to it, on sound principles, have been always ready to bear their testimony.

In conclusion, Gentlemen, I may be allowed to congratulate the inhabitants of this metropolis, and the nation in general, on the establishment of this Institution in a city which, though it is the most wealthy, and one of the largest in the world, has, until within these last two years, been one of the few European capitals in which there has existed no great general school of learning. I may also venture to express my satisfaction, in common with your own, as to the general and liberal principle on which this University has been founded; namely, that of disclaiming all dictatorial and all coercive interference with regard to Religion. It has the honour of setting the first example, in England, of an institution of this kind in which no tests, no subscriptions, no religious disabilities whatever, form any part of the system; and in which persons of every sect, and every name, and every denomination are equally eligible to all its advantages. It is the first to recognise, in its entire extent, the great principle that man has no right to inflict any civil and social privations, the privation of education in particular, on his fellow-man, as an orderly member of the community, on account of his private opinions on the subject of Religion, which, as it is a subject of the highest moment, and the highest sacredness, is degraded from its celestial dignity and grandeur by being made the watchword of political, and party, and secular interest; and which ought to be arbitrated solely at the highest of all tribunals—the tribunal of the Creator and Governor of the world; who alone has the right and the power of punishing for mental error, and to whom alone man can, in this respect, be responsible.

Had religious profession and belief always been left to argument and persuasion—to the jurisdiction of conscience, and the conviction of truth—had Christianity been trusted to make its own way by its own weapons—had it been left to make its appeal to men solely on the ground of another and a future existence, instead of being made, to a great extent, an element of mere secular and political interest, I am persuaded that half and more than half of that virulence and rancour which is too well known by the name of the *odium theologicum*, would have failed to embroil communities, and to mar that charity without which religion is but an empty sound.

More especially, to throw any sectarian or political barrier in the way of man's acquiring the common boon of knowledge, on the supposition of his being in error, is like depriving him of the light of heaven. It is at once to reproach him with being in darkness, and to exclude him from the light. It is nothing less than to visit him with a kind of moral and spiritual inquisition; and to direct against him a thunder not less formidable or less unjust than that of the Vatican itself; for it is, as far as possible, to lay the whole region of his mind under an interdict, and to pronounce an anathema on all his faculties.

Though the term *persecution* is usually associated with the dungeon and the torture, the scaffold and the flame, and is regarded as a name for error armed with power against truth, yet we may safely include under the idea of persecution, all privations, all pains, all disabilities, which are inflicted on account of religious opinions *as such*, even supposing that the given opinions be false or erroneous in their principles. The smaller punishment is as truly persecution as the greater; the difference is only in degree; and in both cases the infliction is alike marked by folly, by injustice, and by presumption;—by presumption, in laying claim to a prerogative which does not, and cannot belong to man,—that of punishing for demerit, or supposed demerit, which is of such a nature as not to come within the sphere of his jurisdiction; by injustice, in denying the full right of private judgment, which belongs equally to all; and by folly, in acting on the principle that error can be annihilated and truth promoted, by holding out motives which must always fail of producing honest conviction and sincere belief; since these, from the very constitution of the human faculties, can never be constrained from without, but must altogether result from the weight of evidence upon the mind.

To these general views, permit me to add, that it is not on the ground that it is of no consequence to man, as an accountable being, what be his *religious belief*, that I advocate the principle of *freedom from all human coercion* in regard to it—the general principle on which this Institution rests: on the contrary, I regard man as responsible for the moral state of his mind which leads to his religious belief—responsible to the Creator and Governor of the world, and to him alone; and this in proportion to the light and the evidences which are placed within his reach. I advocate these general principles from a persuasion that they are the only ones which harmonize with the imperfection of human nature, with the common rights of man, and with the spirit and design of religion itself; nor can I doubt but that they must increasingly prevail as knowledge advances.

That these principles, fairly acted on, should be amenable to the charge which has been so industriously, and so repeatedly, and with so much prejudice to this Institution brought against them—the charge of leading to irreligion and *Infidelity*—I must confess myself at a loss to perceive: and did I feel, Gentlemen, that, by any conduct of mine, I could be regarded as rendering myself justly obnoxious to such an imputation—that I was contributing in any way to obscure that only and illustrious light which has been given to man to guide him to a future, and a higher and a nobler state of being than the present—could I conceive that, however insignificant in itself my agency might be, I was doing any part towards undermining the sublimest, and the only hopes of man that are worthy of the name, and without which all the cultivation of his intellect, and all the advancement of his knowledge, are baseless and perishable as a dream, and have no worthy object, and no grand and sufficient end—I mean his hopes of Immortality, as they are founded on the basis of the Christian Revelation, and on the announcements which it contains, I trust there is no sacrifice that I should not stand ready to make at what I believe to be the shrine of Truth; where alone, I am convinced, lie deposited those motives, those aids, and those sanctions which can form any permanent security for morality and virtue in the present life, and any rational and consoling expectation of felicity in the next. I feel persuaded, however, that the principles on which this Institution is founded involve no such consequences.

I cannot but trust that this University, which is so much in keeping with the spirit of the times in which we live, and with the career of Civil and Religious Liberty, and which possesses the merit of subjecting itself to the influence of enlightened public opinion, will go on advancing in prosperity every successive year; and will find the elements of its success in the increased support of the wise and the good; in the harmonious co-operation of all its Teachers in the promotion of its grand general interests; in the justice and the candour with which the principles on which it is founded are examined, more particularly by those classes of the community to whom it may fairly be considered as most entitled to look for patronage and encouragement; and in the absence of whatever can tend, at any time, in reason, to repel the growing confidence even of its most timid friends:

D

so that, while nothing can be construed as interfering with the private efforts of Parents and Guardians, in reference to that religious discipline of which the daily home is the appropriate scene, the general preparation of youth for stations of usefulness and honour in society may be secured, on the broad fundamental principle of rejecting, within the walls, all party distinctions, and of adopting the impartial motto of the Carthaginian queen :

" Tros Tyriusque mihi nullo discrimine agetur."

THE END.

LONDON:
PRINTED BY THOMAS DAVISON, WHITEFRIARS.

www.ingramcontent.com/pod-product-compliance
Lightning Source LLC
Chambersburg PA
CBHW081307040426

42452CB00014B/2684